HOW TO MAKE MONEY WITH AMAZON AFFILIATE MARKETING

THE ULTIMATE STEP-BY-STEP GUIDE TO MAKING MONEY FROM HOME (OR ANYWHERE IN THE WORLD)

MICHAEL GREENE

CONTENTS

INTRODUCTION

The Internet is a haven of opportunities; however, since anyone can have easy anonymity, it has also becomes a nest for scammers. Among the most famous scams are the countless programs that promise to give financial freedom to anybody who signs up. As expected, quite a number of people were lured and paid the membership fees just to gain access to the information on how to achieve the promised success, but only to find out they were given nothing of value and the program is just earning from their membership fees, which mostly are monthly recurring charges. We can see a lot of these people post on blogs, forums, and social media sites how they were being ripped off by these scammers.

However, out of this heap of Internet money-making programs, Amazon Affiliate Marketing stood out. It has been receiving positive feedback and recommendation from online marketers and has become a topic in entrepreneurial news sites. Amazon Affiliate Marketing is not a get-rich-quick scheme, but with the right investment on time and effort, a person can earn enough to maybe quit one's job—but, of course, it won't happen overnight.

THE ADVANTAGES OF AMAZON AFFILIATE MARKETING

Affiliate marketing is a method that allows a person to earn a commission by referring other people's products and services. Amazon Affiliate program is a marketing tool by the online store giant, Amazon.com, to drive traffic, specifically customers, to the site. It was introduced to the public in 1996 and became one of the first online platforms in affiliate marketing. After 17 years, it is still helping online sellers, affiliate marketers, bloggers, website developers, and product reviewers make money by posting links on their website leading to an Amazon product, usually related to the content of the site. When visitors clicked on this link and purchased *anything* on Amazon, the website owner gets a commission from the sale.

Aside from the commissions, there are a lot of reasons why one should become an Amazon affiliate. Here are the top six reasons:

1. *It is legitimate.* It is a program by a trusted name in online marketing, Amazon.com. They have an A+ rating from Better Business Bureau, a

guarantee that there is no hideous text in the fine print.

2. *It is for free.* Membership fees are usually the barrier between interested and willing people and money-making programs. If you scout the web for ways on how to make money online, most of the programs have a hefty membership or subscription fee. It is frustrating to have to pay something before you can earn. With Amazon Affiliate Marketing, you can sign up even with a zero balance in your account.

3. *Amazon Affiliate marketing tools are simple and easy to use.* The creators of the program understand that not all entrepreneurs have good technical skills, so they made sure their program is simple enough to be used by anybody. In fact, basic computer and Internet skills are just what you need. Tasks can be done with a click of the mouse.

4. *There is more than one option for the payment method.* Most money-making programs pay their affiliate through check or with a third-party payment processor, like PayPal. These payment methods take a long time. With Amazon Affiliates, members can choose if they want to collect their earnings through direct deposit, check, or Amazon gift card.

5. *Amazon almost has any product you can think of.* The wide variety of product categories gives affiliates a lot of options in choosing a target market. Plus, there are a lot of products in each category, which means more options and recommendations.

6. *There's no other program that has the same track record of successful affiliates.* There are already people whose Amazon-affiliated websites are giving them an earning of six-digit figure a year. The good thing about this community is most of them are willing to answer newcomers' concerns.

With all these good things about Amazon Affiliate Marketing, signing up for the program is *not* your first priority. You first need to have a place to promote the products, which means creating a website. The website's information is also needed when signing up.

If you already have an existing website, it is good news; however, you must evaluate if it has decent content—that is, if it contains informative and interesting posts and not a rant about how you hate your boss. Too personal musings may make visitors uncomfortable clicking on your promotional links. If you have a diary-like blog, consider making a new one. If you already have good traffic on that site, it may hurt, but you may want to save your posts and revamp the site for a new and non-personal theme. But if you don't want to change a single thing about your blog and would just like to put in Amazon links, it's still fine. Again, it's your choice. However, creating a new one just for the affiliate marketing program is still the best option.

STRATEGIES TO FINDING YOUR NICHE MARKET

Before creating a website, you should first think of what it would be all about. It's not a good idea to go all out and feature random stuff. Start-up websites that don't have a themed content have a higher percentage of failing to drive traffic to the site. The site would have very limited content about a specific product, meaning when people search for a product that you have posted about, your page would not end up on the first page of the Google results. There is a very slim chance that your site gets clicked and an even slimmer chance for your Amazon promotional links. Always remember that the better the traffic, the better the sales.

A niche market is a group of people that have similar lifestyle characteristics, purchasing behavior, hobbies, and interests. Niche marketing, also known as micromarketing, is the narrowing down of the population to a specific market (niche market) so businesses can concentrate all their efforts on delivering this market's needs. Though concentrated on just one segment of the consumer community, niche marketing is proven to have higher customer conversion rate because your market is already interested with your content or products.

An example of niche marketing is organic food. So instead of making a website about food, which is too vast a topic, you go with specific type of food, targeting people living the healthy life.

Here are tips and strategies on how to find a niche market.

1. *Interests.* This is the easiest way to find a topic for your website because you know the topic so well. For example, if you are into golf, creating a website about it is an advantage because you know what types of information and products the beginner and professional golfers are looking for. It would be easier for you to write engaging and informative contents and interact with the visitors.

2. *Job-related.* If you've been in your job for quite a time now that you know it inside out, then you can talk about it in your site. For example if you're an illustrator, you can give tips and tricks about it. For your promotional links, you can feature the devices that you are using or review the latest illustration software released. The readers know your expertise through your posts so they will trust your recommendations.

3. *Educational-background related.* Whatever field you're studying, as long as you can make good content about it, consider making it your theme. For example, if you're a horticulture student, blog about plants. Educate visitors how to grow them, what's the best time of the year to plant

them, etc. Since you're an expert in the field, make recommendations on what products to use and add the Amazon affiliate links.

4. *Trends.* If you're feeling competitive and adventurous and want to know where people are *mostly* spending their money, you can search for the latest trends. Although there are programs that help you identify the top things people search for on Google, it is not necessary to purchase these programs. The easiest and cost-effective way to do it is to check Amazon Bestsellers. It has all the popular products, from electronics, home improvement, clothing, books, jewelry, and even computer softwares. Out of these categories, you can choose one and maybe make a review site about it.

Once you've picked a topic, do a little check on Google on how many websites are already up and running with the same theme or content as yours. For example, if you decided to take on "car accessories," there are more than 233 million sites that talk about it. A little narrowing would help. If you use "mounted bike racks," the number of site would go down to 3 million, which is still a huge number. Try other related searches, like "car floor trashstand litter bag," which would only give you 72 thousand sites. Creating contents about specific products, like "car floor trashstand litter bag," would give you a much higher chance of appearing on the first page of Google results.

AN INEXPENSIVE WAY TO CREATE A TRAFFIC BOUND WEBSITE

Two of the most common website platforms are WordPress and Blogger. Though WordPress came in late, four of six websites use it, including huge organizations such as Forbes, CNN, and eBay. WordPress is the top choice because: First, WordPress is very easy to set-up, taking only a couple of minutes. Second, when it comes to customization, it rocks. It has a lot of designs, which a lot is for free, to cater different industries. You can have a professional-looking website without purchasing a theme. Fourth, WordPress automatically shrinks and creates the mobile version of your site, making sure it still looks good on smaller screens.

Below is the step-by-step guide of creating a website for less than $25.00. All third-party websites and providers used here are chosen because they are the best in terms of price and quality.

GETTING **a Website Host and Creating a Domain Name**

A website host is a business providing storage space for

your data so it can be accessed by anybody in the web. For example, if you upload photos on Facebook, you are basically uploading this photo to Facebook's computer so it can be accessed by your friends with the use of the Internet. Hosting costs an average of $8 to $10 a month.

A domain name is the www.YourWebsitesName.com. You can choose any website name—as long as it is not yet taken. Most of the time, the website title is also used as the website domain for people to easily remember it. Domain name costs an average of $12 annually.

Website hosting and domain name can be from the same provider. We will use Hostgator as our provider.

Creating a Web Host Account

1. Go to www.hostgator.com and click on the "Web Hosting" tab.

Hostgator has three basic plans: Hatchling Plan ($7.16/month), Baby Plan ($7.96/month), and Business Plan ($11.96/month). Hatchling plan only supports a single domain; Baby and the Business plans can have unlimited domains. The main difference between Baby and Business plans is that the Business plan comes with a free toll-free number.

As you can see, the best option is to go with Baby Plan.

1. Click on "Order Now" under the Baby Plan package.
2. Register a domain name.

The next page will ask you to enter your domain name.

If you have a Hostgator coupon code, type it in the coupon code box to get a discount. There are a lot of available Hostgator coupon codes on the Internet. You can easily find one. These are from the Hostgator affiliates.

Click "Continue."

1. Double check your package plan, which should be Baby Plan, and the total percent of the discount from your coupon code, if you have any.
2. Fill in the billing information. If you're from the United States, you can use your credit card for the payment. Otherwise, you can use PayPal.
3. Click "Create Account."

You will receive a confirmation of your registration after a couple of minutes in your e-mail. This e-mail has all the important links and information, such as username and password, so be sure not to delete it.

INSTALLING **WordPress**

When you receive the e-mail, click on the Control Panel link. It will ask you for a username and a password. You can get this information from the same e-mail.

1. On the Control Panel, scroll down to Software/Services.
2. Click on "Quick Install" icon.
3. On the left side of the next page, under Blog Software, click on "WordPress." It will give you the WordPress information. Just click on "Continue."
4. Click on your domain on the drop-down box.

All of your domain names are listed here if you already have multiple websites.

5. Fill out the information needed. Make sure your e-mail address is correct. For the blog title, you can put in anything; anyway, it can be changed later.

6. Click "Install Now."

7. Take note of the username and password the system gives you when it's done installing. It will be used later.

8. Wait for 2 to 4 hours. The message that the comes with the username and password says the installation is ready, but your website is actually still not working because it will take a minimum of 2 hours and a maximum of 4 hours before the system can put everything in place.

LOGGING **in to WordPress Admin Account**

After four hours, go back to where you left off and click on the link where it says your website will be accessed. When the site is already up, you need to login to your account.

Type in YourWebsitesName.com/wp-admin. This will ask for the username and password given by the system earlier after the WordPress installation. Fill in the information and log in.

INSTALLING A THEME

Under Appearances, click Themes. You can sort themes according to what's trending, popular, or newest.

You can also sort it by its free or premium category. When you hover your mouse over the theme, if it is for free, you can either activate or preview it. For premium themes, purchase and preview options will show. Once you activate your theme, you can customize settings such as header, fonts, and backgrounds.

CREATING **Contents for Your Website**

The secret to get good traffic no matter how many times Google changes its policy on page ranking—because it always do—is to create compelling, informative, and unique content. A lot of website owners and developers overlooked it and focused instead on other techniques. Well, search engine optimization such as keywording works, but not for a long time, because after a Google-policy change, the keywording technique used may no longer be applicable. There have been a lot of Amazon affiliates reporting going down in their Google ranks, subsequently decreasing the number of visitors and sales, each time Google changed their policy in their effort to promote more quality contents.

Here are steps on how to create quality contents for you site.

1. Write a list of your topics that revolve around your niche market.

You can start from what the website is all about, its mission and vision, if there are any, and move forward to other related topics. For example, if your website is all about reusable office supplies, you can write posts about the world's pollution problem, tips on how to reuse office supplies, events and organizations that promotes recycled products, information on how many hectares of land will be saved from landfills if we are to reuse products, stores where one can have great deals on recycled products, trivia, how to minimize office supply use, and many more.

1. Determine if you are to write the content or outsource the job.

If you are a writer by heart and if you have enough time on your hand, you can write the contents yourself, but if you're the kind of person who always find a hard time gathering your ideas and translating your thoughts into words or you're just plain busy, hire a content writer. Elance and oDesk are two of the sites where you can find a contractor that will do an excellent writing job for you for a very affordable price. Just make sure to check the contractor's job history.

1. Don't make articles too long or too short.

Too short articles feel rushed and have too little information; too long articles are skipped. Keep your articles around 350 to 700 words.

1. Proofread articles.

Nothing turns off a visitor more than misplaced commas, small letters at the beginning of the sentence, and thirteen punctuation marks at the end. It gives the impression of poor quality.

1. Make sure the contents are original.

Google has a policy against plagiarism. Whenever their system finds that your content is a duplicate, it penalizes it by lowering it down the rank or, worse, never putting it in the search results.

1. Determine how many times a week the website gets updated.

What your website is all about plays a big role on your post frequency. If you're writing about the latest news around the world, then it requires to be updated every day. If you talk about yoga, bestseller books, or home remodeling, then three times a week is already a good number. Be consistent with the posting time.

1. Add related pictures on the page. It adds appeal to your content and aesthetics to your page. Cite pictures' sources correctly.

CREATING AN ACCOUNT WITH AMAZON AFFILIATE MARKETING PROGRAM AND EARNING MONEY

With your website up and running, it is time to create an Amazon Affiliate account. Below are the steps on how to register to become an affiliate:

1. Go to Amazon.com.
2. Scroll down to the bottom of the page. You will find a link that says, "Become an Affiliate." Click on that link. It will ask for your e-mail address.
3. Fill in your name and address. Be sure that it is your real name and correct address because this information will be used for your checks or direct deposits.
4. Set your payment method. If you're from the United States, it is best to select direct deposit. Funds will reach your account 7 to 15 days earlier than checks. You need to have $10.00 earnings before Amazon can send you your money. Amazon will need your bank's name; the type of account, whether it's a savings or a

checking account; your bank's account number;
and your bank's routing number. If you like to
be paid by check, there is a $15.00 charge.

If you're from outside United States, direct deposit is
not an option, and check payment has the minimum payout
of $100.00; however, the $15.00 fee will be waived.

1. On the next page, fill out website information.
    Information needed are the name of your
    website, where your Amazon affiliate ID will be
    based; the URLs or addresses of websites you
    will use to send traffic to Amazon, which can
    include your personal or your website's social
    media sites; a description of what your site is all
    about; and your reason for joining Amazon's
    affiliate program, which you can choose one
    from the drop-down box.
2. Select products you want to advertise. You will
    be routed to a page where tutorials and other
    marketing tools can be found on the left side of
    the screen and a long search box on the middle.
    This is where you find products you want to
    advertise on your website. For example, if you
    type "reusable office materials," you will get
    more than 2,000 products.
3. Get links. On the right of the product name and
    prize, you will see a tab that says "Get Link."
    Once you click on this tab, it will give you
    option on how you want the product to appear
    on your site—whether you want it to be just an
    image, plain text, both image or text, or in a
    widget. Copy the HTML code provided below

the design you choose and paste it on your site. When somebody visits your site, reads your content, clicks the link you posted, and purchases something on Amazon, you'll be earning your first dollar.

FINDING PROFITABLE PRODUCTS IN AMAZON

Though there is an abundance of products for any niche market imaginable in Amazon, it is wise to sort through the heap. You can't just put any product links you want on your website and cross your fingers that it might interest readers.

Evaluating your targeted market should be the first thing to do in considering a product. Research what problems your audience has. What are their needs? What are their pain points and challenges? What are their desires? What products they have a hard time looking? Remember, niche marketing is providing the needs of a group of people.

Below are some ways you can dig deeper into your niche market's needs:

1. Forums

There is no better way to know your niche market's needs than reading their firsthand experience, concern, and sentiments in forums. People post on forums to get information or advice—just the thing you're looking for.

1. How-to Websites

How-to websites give you an idea what are the things your niche market wants to know about. For example, if we will go back to our reusable office supplies, how-to websites will tell you what office supplies can be repurposed and what other materials needed to do such.

1. Popular blogs

Check popular blogs that has the same niche market as yours. Use their contents to generate new ideas.

1. Asking friends that belong to your niche market —both offline and online.

Asking them does not necessarily mean popping the question of "What do you need?" You can do this by allowing comments and discussion on your contents. People easily spill their opinions, which are mostly based on experience and needs, if you give them the space. Do the same on the website's social media page.

HOW TO MAKE THE PRODUCTS SELL

Aside from the generic posts on your website, writing reviews can significantly increase your sales. Studies show that reviews are more effective than a full-length sales page. It is because readers will let their guard down when they know they are not reading a material from a person who's trying to sell them something.

There are three kinds of format that you can choose in creating product reviews.

1. Single product review

A single product review is not a promotion. You should not be glowing with your praise about the product or it will create warning signs in the reader's brain that you're an affiliate promoting the product. Of course, you should also not overkill it with the cons. Present both positive and negative in a neutral way. You are there to help your visitors decide. At the end of the review, make your stand whether it is a product you will buy or not.

1. Comparison review

There will always be that two brands which are closely competing. These are the types of products that interested individuals usually look for reviews online because they can't just make up their mind on which to buy. The review's goal is to present what features of the products are similar and highlight the difference. Cite what one product has that the other doesn't have and explain briefly the advantage of such feature. At the end of the review, share your recommendations.

1. Chart-type review

This type of review is popular among the type of products that have a lot of features and a lot of good brands competing. An example of this is technology products, like smartphones. Three or more products are reviewed at the same time. Features would be listed, and each product will get a checkmark if it has the feature and an X mark if otherwise. Recommendations would be based on the results.

Is a Brief Review or a Long Review Better?

The good news is: brief reviews convert to sales better than full-page reviews. It is because the article is short and readers will have the time to read it. It is straight to the point, making it easier to understand and compel readers. If you give them a link to Amazon right after the crisp introduction, they will most likely click on your link to check further information and other reviews about the product.

IS IT **Necessary to Use the Product Before Creating a Review?**

Reviews are expected to be written by people who have used the product. It's more of a testimonial that the product works, or not, as advertised. So, should you use products first before actually creating reviews about them? The answer to this is: You should if you can. However, this is not practical, especially with expensive items. You don't need to buy a phone for $300.00 just to review it.

You can research about customer reviews and feedbacks. Listen to what the people who have really used the product are saying. Read the product's sales page. Check for complaints posted in forums. From there, create your own review. Again, make sure not to copy any of the contents you've read as your audience might already have read one of those reviews.

ULTIMATE STRATEGIES TO MAXIMIZE EARNINGS

Amazon Affiliate Marketing links are powerful. They generate money for you even if you're sleeping. It is just right to get the most out of it after all the hard work you've done creating your website. Below are some techniques on how to maximize your income from the links.

1. *Cross merchandise.* Your visitors would be interested in a wide variety of products. For example, if you're creating a review about a certain camera, feature other cameras on the page.
2. *Evaluate orders report.* Amazon will give you a report on which products customers bought after clicking on your link. If they bought something you did not advertise, consider directly promoting these products on your website.
3. *Promote higher-priced products.* The higher the sale, the higher the commission.

4. *Check link's performance.* Amazon can generate your links performance reports. From this data, check which links are not working—meaning, not converting to sales—and consider replacing it. Of course, you will not do this after a month since you posted the links. Give it three months. If majority of your links are giving you good sales except for two or three, change it.

5. *Increase link's visibility.* It helps the chance of customers clicking the link if they can easily see it on the page. Customer should not look for it. It is good to place it on top and at the bottom of the post.

6. *Update your featured products, if applicable.* There are products that always have new and updated versions, especially technology-related products. You don't want your links to become obsolete, so update accordingly. However, there are products that even if years have passed, it will continue to sell. For example, books that have been bestsellers for years. As long as it's making profit, you can leave it as it is.

7. *Always, always make sure your links are correct.* Your hard work will go to waste with broken links. Check regularly. Also, make sure that these links contain your Amazon affiliate ID so everything will be credited to your account. However, you don't have to do it manually. It will eat up so much of your time. An Amazon company, Alexa, will help you determine and remove broken links for free. Take advantage of it.

BUILDING FREE QUALITY **Backlinks to Your Website**

BACKLINKS ARE links from other sites going to your website. This is one of the most effective methods to increase traffic in your website and move up in the Google rank search results. There are programs available that create backlinks for you; however, it is always better to go for free and quality backlinks—that is, placing them on free sites and knowing visitors clicked on your link because they are interested with the content that goes with it.

Below are steps on how to build free and quality backlinks:

1. Search niche-related forums and answer questions and concerns with useful information. On your signature, include a link to your website. It is important to just put a link on the signature and not on the post so you will not be tagged as a spammer.
2. Article directories such as Ezinearticles ranks high in Google. Submit niche-related articles to them. On the author's bio or resource page, add the website link.
3. Create press releases and submit them to popular press release websites such as PRNewswire.
4. Create related video content and post it in YouTube. A lot of people watch videos about

things they want to know on YouTube. This popular video site has millions of visitors each day. Take advantage of its traffic. Under your video, lead them to your website through a link.

AFTERWORD

Amazon Affiliate Marketing is wonderful online opportunity that can give you the financial freedom you've been dreaming of, but again you have to put in the required effort. Don't forget to tweak your website every now and then if your judgment sees it right. There are times that the information is too much that you don't know which one to do first. Create a goal and write your actions steps to achieve it. This will help you see clear through the heap of information.

Keep on learning new things. Motivate yourself because you might not be getting good results in the first three months since it can take time to build your site and create traffic on it. Never give up. Consistency is the key. There are countless of successful affiliate marketers online. Read their story. Learn from them. Keep inspired. If they can do it, of course you can—if you want.

To start with this affiliate marketing program, you don't need to quit your job. You can allocate three to four hours on weekdays building your website and your online presence and work on it longer during the weekends. It all depends on you.

The program has been creating thousands of successful online entrepreneurs for more than 17 years. This length of time tells it all. It works, but again, not overnight. You are now on the right path. All you need to do is to take the steps toward your goal.

www.ingramcontent.com/pod-product-compliance
Lightning Source LLC
Chambersburg PA
CBHW071532210326
41597CB00018B/2977